Million Dollar Creator Economy

Rohan Bhardwaj

Published by Rohan Bhardwaj, 2021.

While every precaution has been taken in the preparation of this book, the publisher assumes no responsibility for errors or omissions, or for damages resulting from the use of the information contained herein.

MILLION DOLLAR CREATOR ECONOMY

First edition. September 17, 2021.

Copyright © 2021 Rohan Bhardwaj.

Written by Rohan Bhardwaj.

You Can Earn A Million Dollars In One Year!

If you can convince 1000 people to send you $100 per month for one year.

And that's easy if you have a business – so you can get the $100 per month as a sales figure. But that won't be the profit. Nevertheless – you can squeeze a million dollars in profit by few upsells.

So what's going on – can you realistically make one million dollars or is that number far fetched.

Go and start a lemonade stand – sell it for $2 such that your profit will be $1.

By the end of a month, it is reasonable that you would have sold at least one lemonade per day – so that would be $30 in profit.

Whoever comes to your stand – have a great talk and make sure the lemonade is tasty. They will come back – with friends too.

And new customers will always come up. So you can make about $1000 per year with this strategy.

Now instead of lemonade, try to come up with something more expensive and valuable which people need. And by the means of math, you can understand that you have the formula to earn million dollars.

You just have to test and figure out the jigsaw pieces. Provide value to society, make them come back and at least 1000 people should need your product or service.

And boom you are a millionaire. Do send some of my commission, okay.

Luring New Customers

In this day and age, working at a company doing a routine job isn't something everyone aims for. Even if you do it, you are constantly in search of something you are passionate about. Something which you can do enough times in such a quality that you can survive and thrive.

Thanks to the internet and the amount of information it holds, now nothing is stopping you to access any information.

Wanna code, go to FreeCodeCamp. Wanna sell something to millions, sign up for Amazon. And everything in between. Also with the internet, the doors have been opened. It ain't easy – but the door is open.

You can create anything you want and share it with few people. And if they like they will share it and soon it can reach millions of people.

On the alternative, if the initial batch of people didn't like then you can learn and then create another thing. For example, I create YouTube dance videos. They are bad and only seen by about 10 people. But once in a while, it turns out good and then it reaches 10000 people.

So the access to people isn't something available to a select few.

You have to be generous and boom your work can reach more people than ever before. All you had to do is gain trust and attention, your customers – not all of them but a select few will give you money.

And that's all you need to become an artist. But if you are leaning on the business side of things, then you need to scale – bring in more revenue than last month. And then scale again to become the best in that category.

But at what cost?

Promises

YOUR CUSTOMERS ARE the lifeline of your business. They pay money in exchange of services or goods and you become rich. Customers are happy as long as the value they see is more than the money they pay. Also the story they tell themselves helps in keeping their sanity.

When you go for a new service, a promise is being made. Whatever that is the customer signed up for that.

If you tell the customer service is a phone call away then that is your promise. When the customer calls, don't keep her waiting for more than 1 minute. If you do that then your promise failed and the customer will start looking elsewhere.

Over the period you stay in business, you can change, adapt but your core promises shouldn't be compromised. Because that is the heart of your business.

New Customers

THE EASIEST WAY TO lure new customers is to give them a discounted price. Since you are now churning profit, you can adapt to less profit from new customers.

And sure enough, they show up. But there comes a new challenge – you have made a different set of promises to them. Which is cheap prices. So if in future you increase the price, they will shift to the new company which has lower prices.

Also your loyal, dedicated customers will feel cheated. Because they are the ones paying normal fees for the same service.

You might gain some momentum in the short run from new customers. Overall your business strategy just went out of the window. Old customers can't trust you anymore. And the new customers are on the lookout for the cheapest service provider. So it is just a matter of someone new coming up with an easy switch and cheap prices that all your customers might flock to.

Ideal Plan

THE BEST STRATEGY FOR a business to grow is to give more value to the current customers. Such that they bring you referrals. This way you earn more customers by adding value to the current customer.

This ensures no customer is unhappy because there ain't a divide of old and new. Instead, it is the energy between them to promote because of the best service they have been receiving.

So next time, work on your customers which you have to get new clients. And if you want to play the price game. Then increase the price with the new addition of valued-added services – only for new customers. And old customers get to have the same price for a lifetime.

This way, new customers are encouraged to join now so they can avail of future services at the current price. In short, the earlier you join as a customer the more profitable bargain you receive.

Now go back to luring the new customers. But this time, you know the rule to succeed.

How To Sell Your Soul?

If you want to live on Earth then you need to sell your soul. Life isn't fair, it's harsh and you can't plan it.

Historically, when you think of selling your soul - you think of the devil. Because when you are doing some bad stuff then others will comment - "Have you sold your soul to the devil?"

Because of course when you do bad things, your soul will be punished when you die. And it won't be accepted into heaven. So the only logical conclusion is that the devil has your soul. That's why you are doing the bad stuff. Or you willingly have sold your soul and that's why it doesn't matter if you do bad stuff now. The moral of the story is that your soul is the real you. It's pure - does a good thing and is sacred. Don't sell it, please.

The Salesman At Your Door

SELLING IS AN ART AND as a consume - you want to get all the deals. Best, if someone can explain everything to you. But when you are chilling at your home, a knock from a salesman is an inconvenience. You want to close the door asap however you are reluctant to shut the door in someone's face.

And she begins selling everything from fan to the cooker to voodoo magic. At first, she says it's FREE. Slowly the price starts appearing and before you know it - you have a hat worth $3 bought for $10.

Both of you are happy because you got a new hat. And she got a sale. If you didn't buy anything from her then you don't lose much.

But for her, she has been doing this all day. And no one listened to her. She is tired with no sales. It's time to go back home. And she is hungry. Your payment will help her feed herself.

She has to sell like her life is on the line because it's her life on the line. And at the moment, you realize - when the stakes are high, you don't care. You will be willing to sell your soul if it means food on the table.

You Selling Yourself

LET'S TAKE THE EXAMPLE of a relationship. When you fall in love and are chasing the approval of the opposite sex, you are looking to sell yourself.

And because at the initial stage, you want to somehow get in a relationship - you do anything to get sold. It means you lie, cover-up bad habits and sometimes change yourself so you are good enough for the relationship.

The same thing happens when you apply for an interview. Sure, you need skills but most people have them in your interview lot. So, you need a way to stand out. You do this by selling yourself - your personality, your ideas and the unique you. And if the case is that the job is too much important for you - like no food then you sell your soul to get the job.

If the desperation is revealed, the bad folks can and will take advantage of you. The best bet is to let people have the illusion of you are fine even if you will sell your soul if the time comes.

Hobby, Passion and Selling

LIFE IS UNPREDICTABLE - you can plan all day but life gives you surprises. Let's take the example of many people working who have an education in 'X' but working in the 'Y' industry.

There are many reasons for this - lack of proper education, fewer opportunities and too much competition so you settling for other jobs. Eventually, you are working in a 9 to 5 job which you don't like. And sometimes what you like is not making you money.

However, you can't make this as an excuse to do mediocre work. If you are forcing yourself to do the work you hate, you are selling your soul for money. And that's fine.

But you should try to look for other benefits and learning experiences in your current environment - that way you will feel less stressed out. And you should always work on your passion on the side to make it work. Once, it does - you can stop selling your soul and focus on doing the work that you love.

Sell Your Soul

Seriously, how to sell your soul. If all goes right, you shouldn't. Also, if you are in a position of privilege then don't create situations for others in which they need to compromise.

Selling your soul means you are breaking, doing with pain and feels wrong to you. That's not how you should live your life.

And if you are in such a situation, work hard on weekends, upgrade yourself, connect and try to come out of it.

You don't have to love your job but it doesn't have to crush your soul either.

How To Connect With Your Fans

A nd help everyone in the process...

Benefits Of Social Media

FACEBOOK HAS MORE THAN a billion people on them. That's an astounding number. It means, no matter your target audience – you will always find someone who is on Facebook.

One way to grow on Facebook is to create a page. Initially, when Facebook was new – they approached the companies and asked them to create pages. Because the companies had fans so they can like their page. And once you have followers on your page, you rule. Now companies can make a post and it will show up on the feeds of all people who have liked your page.

It was a win-win situation for everyone. Facebook has ads all over so they always earn money. The companies got an easy way to reach all of their fans. You post something and it shows up on their feed. And fans got the message from the brands they like. And everything was fair. If you don't like a brands post, you can hide – or remove your like.

Facebook started promoting pages to creators. So many creators who were new jumped to Facebook and shared posts, advertised, brought fans from other platforms. And then built an amazing connection with their audience.

Again, everyone won – the creator got a hassle-free way to reach their fans on their feed. Fans loved seeing posts from creators. And Facebook was getting money from ads. Again everyone was happy and the game was fair.

Things once in a while would go viral on social media. And then it would bring new fans and sales along. The very genesis of social media is virality. If enough people like your post, it is shown to their friends too and so on. It creates a chain. So there was a natural hidden gem in social media pages. Your post could go viral – once in a while.

After almost everyone was on Facebook and they had made effort to have thousands and millions of followers – Facebook did an unfair move.

They started limiting post reach when a brand page would make. For example, if your page has 10,000 followers. Your post will be shown to just 100 people. Citing it was for a better user experience. Which is a lie. Because if someone doesn't like your post, they can hide or even unlike a page to stop following you.

You asked Facebook what is happening – what's the use of having 10,000 followers when you can't reach them. And they provided with a solution – pay money and they will show them to the users.

If they really cared about user experience, they wouldn't show the post for anything. But that was just a ploy to get money from you. And now you are stuck, you have to build your business on Facebook, your fans are expecting a post from you. And now if you don't pay, you would have to literally start from the beginning.

Although social media has and will provide benefits to you. Eventually, it all depends on their mood and what they think is right. Your business can go out of business if you rely heavily on social media.

First, they lure you, then trick you and then ask you to pay. It's all about making loads of money. That's why you should use social media as a secondary or tertiary route. And not your primary method. Else, you will always be on the ledge. And you can fall anytime the owner of the social media doesn't like you.

Also, there are other issues like when social media is biased. And they want your post to reflect a certain bias. You will be forced to do that or else limit your exposure.

YouTube has dictated what is right as per them. And now YouTubers have to do exactly that or they will face issues like less money or less reach or sometimes both.

The only type of videos you will see on trending is when it's not controversial. Because YouTube is making policies in line with the advertiser's bias. So they might proclaim that they are a creators platform, instead, they are an advertising platform. And you are there to fill in the gap. And slowly, you as a creator is losing value because almost all companies are on YouTube. Even if all creators shut their accounts – it won't affect YouTube.

YouTube lured creators to make YouTube the biggest platform. And then they welcomed corporate and now creators have been sidelined.

Always, keep a backup plan when your whole career is dependent on one social media. Because most YouTubers have no option. Video hosting is expensive. So it is a good idea to build a second business irrespective of YouTube with your YouTube leverage. So you are safe when YouTube tries to fail you.

Disguise But Social Media

THERE ARE MANY WEBSITES which pop up. And they promise you to reach and money. For example, HubPages, Medium and many more.

And when you write on them – you realize they have a structure to help you, a community to feel close in and growth like none. You work hard, write articles and make an impact. You write comments, reply and be a part of the community. Slowly, you have followers which you have earned. Now, they get your articles in your feed because they follow you.

Slowly, when you have convinced many others to join the platform, they have grown big. Now, they don't need you. So they partner with big companies to make content. And only their content shows up in the feed. Now, if you stop creating they don't care. You have made others a habit to go to their platform. And now, they can meet their content needs from others.

You don't matter. Even if you write something, they will not show it to all your followers. Instead, they will introduce a recommended feature. And unless they recommend you, your article won't show to your followers or beyond. For that recommendation, you have to follow their arbitrary rules. Which doesn't exist before? You are forced to do as they wish or leave the platform.

You are now back to square one. So, remember, there might be platforms that might promote you but they will be just another social media.

Always, have your home. A personal website, blog on hosting of your choice. And email connection so you don't have any worry about things to go out overnight. And you can use other platforms as a promotional thing. So go on Medium or HubPages or Twitter. But as a promotional thing and not as your main thing.

Use social media to get fans to your website or blog. And your personal newsletter. Collect their emails. So you can use an email client to email them anything you promised. And they can view them in their email inbox. This is the best user experience too. Because fans willingly buy in the newsletter. And if they don't like what you are sending, they can unsubscribe.

You are safe too. Tomorrow, if Twitter goes out of business or any other social media business. You are safe. Because people often don't change email addresses and if Gmail goes out of business. All you have to do is an email asking for their new email id. You still have the connection. You can email your fans their preferred way.

The medium doesn't allow you to send a message to all your fans. Nor do Linkedin or Twitter or Facebook. When you have an email address, you can email all your fans. There are 2 sides – first, you have the connection control so your emails reach all your fans inboxes. Because people don't change email client and email client hardly goes out of business. And even if it does – you can email your fans before the deadline, ask for their new email id. And boom, your business still rocks.

Emails Are Like Phone Numbers

EMAIL IS THE BEST CONNECTION you can have with your fans. Phone numbers once shared – it becomes difficult to share it again. You don't want to change your phone number. Because you have shared it with everyone. And someone might call on your number. Maybe they have just your phone number and nothing else.

So, when you get a phone number, you keep them. Maybe over the years, you might take in new numbers. But you will keep your old number active.

The same is the case with email ids. You have shared your email id with a bunch of places. And so you don't want to change them. Sure, you might get new email ids over the years. But you will not shut down any email ids you own.

You can change social media but you keep your email. So, if you have to build a fan following based on your leadership, email rocks.

Your fans might change the social media, check it less. And also, social media controls the reach. But with email, you can send emails at your convenience. And your fans will open them at their convenience. Also, your fans will check their email ids often.

Email is a personal, anticipated and welcomed newsletter from the people you admire.

The key here is to use this privilege with care. Don't spam, use the connection to send emails that are useful and keep your promise.

Most of the companies go wrong when they stop keeping up their promise. It doesn't have to be big. But whatever it is, you have to keep it. For example, you can make a promise to share good recommendations. So do that. You can make a promise to give stellar customer service. So doesn't matter how big or small you become, keep that promise.

A promise when made and kept – will help you succeed. And if it doesn't, it will translate as a useful thing to do in your next venture.

One to One Connection

ONE TO ONE CONVERSATION is gold. When your friend sends you something, it's personal. And you feel the connection. Somehow when you write something on social media, it's public. Literally, everyone can see them. And your reaction is public.

But when you send an email, it is personal. Although it is sent to many people. It's as if – all of them are like a single-minded individuals. Because the ideas resonated and hence, all of them have chosen to receive your email.

It's not public. Your fans can reply and it is sent to one person. It's an amazing feeling. Therefore, there is less rage, hatred and more love when the connection happens over email.

Take the example of the Convert company. They help you send emails to your fans. They are a big proponent of plain text emails. Because when your friends send an email, it isn't some image-heavy and bright colours. It's text, it's meaningful and there is a story. Convertkit takes care of the outer appearance of your email. You as a creator need to take care of what goes inside.

When you email your fans, check for any typos. See the story, what's in it for them. Also, don't be pushy. Give, give and give. And then maybe ask one time. That's how a relationship is built in modern-day internet time. You don't lure your fans into giving you an email address to scam them. You want them to grow, succeed and make an impact.

Give so much value that they can't comprehend what's going on. And then ask for something once. You will be surprised by the disproportionate high returns.

But it's not that. You thought of the long-term, you thought about your fans. You thought about the connection.

Email Conversation Is Personal, Anticipated & Welcomed

WHEN YOU BUY STOCK of companies – it might happen that you will have some news. Which will guarantee that a certain stock with skyrocket. And if that happens, the only logical conclusion is to buy all the stock you can from the company. And then after 10 years, you can reap the rewards. But none of this is true. The chances of this happening are almost zero. That you might get struck by lightning than you will get news of such stock. Often it is when things have gone out of hand that you get to know about it.

Take the example of bitcoin – for the longest time, no one believed in it. Those who hold the stocks were either rich already or the ones who were thinking about getting something out of it. Maybe spend to get a pizza.

Only when the bitcoin prizes exploded you got to know about it. And then you tried to catch the wave by investing. But it was already too late. It often it.

The best strategy is to diversify your investments. Maybe you believe in a particular stock, buy few other promising stocks too. That way, your chances of doomsday will go down.

When you are building your presence online – having everything on social media is a big problem. Buy a domain name from one company, host it on another. And collect email addresses from a lead company. And send emails from another email service provider. That way you will have leverage in every form. Also, the most important piece of information – the email address is stored with 2 companies on your behalf. Also, make a backup every month just in case.

If everything has to fail, an email will be the last one to fail. And social media will be the first. Because social media keeps changing. They might introduce one feature and remove one. You have no control. You have to follow their norms.

Many entrepreneurs have stated that the biggest mistake they have made is not capturing the email address when they started. And essentially, building a connection economy.

Here is a quote from Seth Godin on the value of connection and its relation to apparent success:

Put your idea into a format where it will spread fast. That could be an ebook (a free one) or a pamphlet (a cheap one–the Joy of Jello sold millions and millions of copies at a dollar or less).

Then, if your idea catches on, you can sell the souvenir edition. The book. The thing people keep on their shelf or lend out or get from the library. Books are wonderful (I own too many!) but they're not necessarily the best vessel for spreading your idea.

And the punchline, of course, is that if you do all these things, you won't need a publisher. And that's exactly when a publisher will want you! That's the sort of author-publishers do the best with.

If you have connections – email addresses of your fans. Then you already have the biggest thing you need. Rest is just a checklist and you are a success.

How To Create An Awesome Membership Website?

A guide to being generous, lead and make a difference. By sharing what you know and how.

Creating value, offering services and building products. And also make a living at the same time. The Internet makes it fast for you to do this thing. You are required to lead.

What Is A Membership Website

HAVING A BLOG ONLINE is sorta mandatory. Earlier when there used to be only a few extensions available, like com, in, org – the names were limited. Because all the popular ones were taken and you couldn't get your name or something good enough when you start your website.

Some people hoard domain names to cash in when someone is looking for a specific domain name. This happened to the point that the only names available were the ones with random letters.

Thankfully, there are many new extensions that have been released. And the hope is it keeps on releasing slowly so that people willing to buy a domain name get a decent one.

This hoarding of domain names leaves people with less money. They have to settle for whatever they can get their hands on. Internet was build for democracy, but the people with money can simply buy a domain name of their choice. Everyone is in a race to get their online identity. And it's getting difficult to feel like you are doing something new.

When the internet came, it was promised as a new way of doing things. Blogs were few, and not everyone was online. Now, everyone writes online in some form of social media. And everyone owns some sort of blog. It's similar to the diary. It started like that.

And slowly, people started writing about their passion, to share and make an impact. Blogs are everywhere.

If you spend enough time on the internet, you realize you can make money off the internet. Many blow owners are earning millions. And others in hundreds of dollars. Some earn a living, and some receive pocket change.

Naturally, you want to earn money. This is a great thing. There are a few ways to go about it. You can put ads on your blog. But slowly, the earnings from ads have been decreasing. And now, it isn't a recommended way to earn money if you are a solo blogger.

The second is to recommend products and earn a commission if your fans buy the product. That's amazing. But slowly, you can make products yourself and sell them to your fans. Earning good enough money. But what if you can earn money like clockwork every month. That would be amazing. And now you are entering the membership zone.

Either you can offer a section of your website as a paid monthly membership or your whole blog. But you can block your whole blog only when you are already popular. Or you transition from the freemium model to the paid version. The best approach is to write 4 articles per month. And 3 of them would be free. So visitors can come and join your email list. And if they want the 4th article, they can pay a monthly subscription.

Or you can create a paid forum, share exclusive interviews or behind the scenes. All of this is the value you create to provide to your paid member.

A membership website usually has free and paid offerings. And once enough people subscribe to paid, you will earn a consistent income every month.

Different Ways You Can Offer Something

WHAT DO YOU ACTUALLY offer so that some of your fans get convinced to pay you a monthly membership fee?

You can create a podcast that goes on deeper on a topic you covered in an article. So, the idea of the article can still travel. Because it's free. But for someone who wants a deep dive, stories and work that went into understanding a certain topic, you can offer that as a paid value.

Movies often do this. Although their movie is paid, they offer DVDs with extra scenes. So fans of the movie pay even more to get those DVDs.

Or you can create a community. Since you are following a certain blog – you resonate with that person and their ideas. There are others too who are similar to you.

So, a forum can be created, and paid members can be invited. So people who want to interact, go deeper can do so in such paid forums. A community is an awesome paid value.

Another thing you can do is give away the main footage, design or coding – whatever value you provide for free. And behind the scenes, extra footage. So in this way, the people who can't pay still have access to quality material. And die-hard fans get their extra footage for a premium. Everyone is happy.

Or you can connect with your fans. You can make everything you do for free. But every month, you go live with your paid members and interact with them. You are like a mini-celebrity. People will pay to listen to your live stream, your ideas and your raw conversations.

Or you can ask fans to support so you can scale. For example, you can decide 50 per cent of the membership money will be your salary and the other 50 per cent as an investment to make your offering even better. This is amazing because the fans will love to see their money going to improve what is being offered already.

As an extension of this, you can offer your fans to sponsor your work. As a credit, they will get a thank you at the end of work – be it an article or video. You can provide a link to your website to thank everyone who supports you. Avenues are many – membership website is the future in the making. Because this is the most sustainable way to earn money. And the best way to include your fans in your journey. A win-win for everyone involved.

If It's Super Important, It Needs To Be Free

Many people choose a method of membership which is like this – they write 3 articles or make 3 products. They then make 2 free and 1 paid. This seems okay, as long as you are in a niche audience. And your voice won't be needed for a culture shift. But that often isn't true. Your best articles should be free. You have to make memberships on top of that. Like community access or a memory or a thank, you note.

News organizations are jumping into the membership thing. And they are getting a good amount of subscribers. But they are in the news field, which means your news should travel across. Because it's important. If you allow only 1 article per day to free users, then that can be a problem. You won't be making a dent in the culture. Because many people can't pay for everything. So, you should give value in another sense.

For example, a news publisher should make news free for all. But for paid users, they can allow them to comment. A feature is available for members only.

There have been articles that I read and have changed my direction. Those have informed me to make the leap. And if those were behind a paywall, then I would not have been so driven in life.

Internet is an amazing place. Consider the Wikipedia model – it runs on donations. But that donations pay for the senior editors, other employees and an office, apart from running Wikipedia itself. Wikipedia itself is free for anyone to read. Either you can do that, you think of creating a membership website as donations. Which is awesome. Because you keep doing everything the same and die-hard fans pay for you to continue.

Or you can show the extra footage which you never were gonna show as a value to your paid members. Remember, memberships works great. And if you have 1000 true fans paying – you don't need anyone else. You can keep creating things, and you will keep getting those dollars.

But if what you create has to make a dent, in culture and in ages to come – then it has to be available in free form.

Always have a summary of your content publicly available for free. The idea which you want to spread should find a vessel. And in public, is the best vessel.

You might think of these ideas as a contradiction. But the thing is you need to balance. In no way, you should be offering things that are your great work only to paid members. But at the same time, you need to provide enough value in other things – be it access, thank you note or behind the scenes – that they subscribe to your memberships.

Seth Godin does it amazing. He has written extensively on 'The Marketing'. Which is free. Then there is 'The Marketing Seminar', a free video. Then there is a book, 'This Is Marketing' which costs about $20. For someone looking to explore in-depth the marketing. And then there is 'The Marketing Seminar' course which is a membership course. Anyone who is looking to deep dive with a community. So the idea of marketing is given to the public for free. And there are different offerings for various people who want even more.

Own Your Email Subscribers

MEMBERSHIP SITES ARE lucrative. But like in any business – you should own the very thing which is the core. For example, if you are a fashion clothes seller, then you need to protect your business. If you rent a store in a busy location. And slowly over the years, you develop a relationship – your sales keep increasing. But one day, the owner decides to stop renting. And now, you are forced to relocate.

If you haven't built a relationship with the customers, then they will keep buying from that same location. But this time it will be the shop of someone else. You did all the hard work, and now someone else is reaping the benefits. Even worse, you are back to square one – now you have to do all the work again.

If you are a social media influencer, one thing you can do is be on all social media. Because social media have a tendency to go out of business. It has happened before. And there is no guarantee that something new comes and sweeps away your presence.

So whatever new promising thing comes, make an account and mention it on your main social media. Sure, keep doing all the things which you do on your main social media. But keep dropping little bits on other social media accounts which isn't your main account.

And now, if your main social media suddenly decides to shut down itself, then you can redirect your fans to another social media.

Or if your primary social media bans you – you can still do the work because you are active on other social media. So your presence is there. If the ban isn't lifted, you can double down on the next social media, and you will gain enough followers again.

Vine was a short video platform that shut down. But many diverted their audience to YouTube. So when Vine got shut down, they had some traction on YouTube already – so they grew on YouTube. Right now, the upcoming platform is TikTok. Even if you are on Instagram or YouTube, make some presence on TikTok. Divert some fans to TikTok. So if something happens, you can double down on TikTok. And you will gain enough followers because you have the fans to do initial traction.

But what about membership websites. What is something you should do? Remember, no matter what business you are in online. You should own the email subscribers of people who have subscribed to you. And if you use an advance email client, then you may get a segmented list of who had bought something or subscribed to you.

So, if any third party platforms fail or go away or you like something else – you should be able to switch. As long as you own the email lists, you can transport the list and the details. And service like Podia is open to help you export your information and list to you. So you have the liberty to go away any time you like.

But on the other hand, Podia is so awesome that you would like to stay for as long as you create. Podia is literally the creator's paradise. With so many options, it allows you to seamlessly try many things. And also – when you have a complete solution for creators, then why would you try 5 different service providers.

How To Create Value

WITH SO MANY OPTIONS to create value, you will be confused as to what type of value you should create. The first step is to build an audience, so you have enough audience. And then you can build a relationship with them. The best thing is to have a newsletter. No matter which niche or art you are in – you can send a weekly newsletter. Where you can showcase your art, connect and share some tips or nitpicks.

Slowly, you will build a community because you have been giving all the time. And now after a year or so, you can take – start a membership thing.

The best thing to do is to ask your readers, fans, community. Something along the lines, ' Hey, I am thinking to start a membership thing where you pay monthly support. What type of value you would be wanting'.

And then give the option. Via a poll, you can get some idea. And then email 10 fans and share what value you will be giving. Get feedback and then work to have a launch.

After the launch, about 10 per cent of your subscribers should be able to convert. If it's less, then it's okay. But remember to relaunch with a different heading and a variation of the giveaway, sorta like tiers. If you support $3, then you will get a thank you note. If you support $5 then a thank you note and mention it in the newsletter. The aim is to get enough people so you can support yourself. If you get more, then pay it forward – support newsletters that you like and the chain should continue.

This will also boost the economy like none other. Because of the fans support, the big companies would have to innovate.

You can still take sponsors from companies, but they should level up. And provide value to you and your fans. This way, you can get sponsors from amazing companies and make an impact in huge ways. The advertising model would have to convert into a sponsorship model – where they won't track clicks.

They would also need to grow to a connection economy. And the shift in culture would be amazing—something which you propelled too.

From Ads On Blog, Affiliate Income To Membership Subscription From Fans

The future of blogs is here. Also, the road to earning money will become better. Once, the subscription economy of blogs spreads like a fire.

Blogs To Rise

THE INTERNET HAS GIVEN an open ground to everyone. Earlier only reputed newspapers and magazines used to write about their perspective. But now, the doors are open to everyone.

Because blogs have been introduced. You can make one for free, hosted on someone else's server. Or you can buy the hosting and put your domain name on it. Regardless, you can write anything you like.

No one is stopping you, no permission is required. Of course, thousands of people won't flock to your writing the moment you write. But there exists an opportunity. Anyone can use search and land on your writing.

Also, you can share your blogs with friends and they can read and share further. And blogs do get read as much as traditional newspapers and magazines.

Since, everyone can write, start a blog – everyone has done that. And now, there are thousands of blogs on any given topic.

It feels crowded and it is. But that's the price of opening the land of opportunity to everyone. But it's beautiful.

Writing And Earning Money

EARNING MONEY ONLINE is nothing sort of a miracle. And when you earn money from writing, that's whole another world.

But because the internet was new and not too many blogs – earning from writing became an easy endeavour. You were lucky if you were one of the starting breeds. You could have started a blog about anything – write 500 words article and it would rank on the Google search. Which brings you tons of visitors.

And then you can either slap advertisements on your blog or affiliate links. Boom, you can earn a nice paycheck. And therefore, many people earned a lot of money.

But the times have changed. It is no longer an easy thing to write an article and get rankings. There are too many blogs competing for the tiny space. And so does the advertisement industry.

Ad revenue is on the decline because of the bidding system, the middlemen in most cases Google is eating up the bulk of revenue. And you as a user, are left with pennies.

Advertisements can still bring you revenue but you would need millions of visitors for sustainable living. Which would be impossible for the majority of the blog owners.

Google Ads And Others

WHEN IT COMES TO ADVERTISEMENT, Google is the main contender. Initially, when Google started selling ads, it promised a good deal for everybody. You would bid $10 to be placed in one of the blogs. Google would take $2 and the blog owner will earn $2 and you as an advertiser will earn $6. Out of which you will have a profit of $2.

So everyone wins. But when Google started taking up more money while giving less to the blow owners. For example, Google would now take $6 and give $1 to blog owners. You as an advertiser have no choice but to be content with the $3.

Because if you don't advertise then Google will give the spot to the competitor. So regardless of your position now, you are required to keep paying money to stay afloat.

It is similar to the rental game which happened – one of the buildings in prime location gave the location to you for a small rent.

Once you started getting customers, she approached your competitor with statistics of how profitable that is – and sold the location to them.

And the landlord kept doing that, increasing rent and pocketing huge money. And you have no choice but to keep giving money or else your competitor wins and you lose. You will win for pennies – but that's the silver lining, you win. Regardless, the biggest profit keeping giant is the landlord, Google.

Ads Are Dying And They Should

INTERNET USERS HAVE become used to ads such that they don't click on it as often. Or they block the ads in their entirety. So, if you own a blog, it is difficult to earn a good amount of income with ads.

Also, the amount of traffic you would need is mind-boggling. Hence, most people are straying away from ads as their primary source of earning.

Many new avenues exist like affiliate income where you recommend a product or service and earn a commission. Or sell your software, course or membership for valuable content. Hence, this has become the go-to for many blog owners.

The transition has happened where many blog owners have to learn about affiliate marketing, making a course and delivering content in a community so that there be money coming from their writing craft.

But can there be an alternative that doesn't require a writer to juggle all those hats? Yes, if you want to create a course – then good for you. But if you just want to write, can you make a living.

Subscription From Fans

THE BEST WAY TO EARN money is to do so with your direct fans. Let's take an example – if 1000 people read your blog and 100 of them become your fans, you can ask them for a $10 monthly subscription. And boom, you are earning a cool $1000 per month.

And when you grow your fanbase, your earnings will grow too. Unlike advertisements or affiliate income, you don't have to constantly pull in new customers.

All you have to do is make sure your current fan base remains loyal. And doing so is easy. Keep creating content on a regular basis. And ask for feedback on what to change or not.

The best thing about subscription income is that – you don't need millions of visitors to succeed. Hence, many small niche blogs can become successful.

This type of shift didn't happen with advertising. Also, since, you aren't looking to scale much. You can focus on clear writing and taking a stand. You are liable to your fans and not some advertising giant with random rules.

Locked Content

ONE OF THE EASIEST things to do when asking for a subscription is to provide some kind of locked content. For example, many writers write 5 articles a month. But free readers can read only 3 of them. While the paid users can read all the 5 articles.

This way, the writer can earn money. The readers who don't pay get to read some articles. And the super fans who pay up dollars get to read all the articles.

Another way is to lock features like comments and groups. So the free readers get to read all the articles but can't comment or get involved in the group. And the paid audience enjoys every feature.

I am okay with restricting certain features. But I am not a fan of locking articles for giving them a bonus to the paid users.

Coming from a poor background, paying for articles isn't something I could do instantly. And as Seth Godin says, if what you are saying is important then don't put it behind the paywall. The best approach is to give access to other things like emoji access in comments or access to private groups for discussion.

But the ideas in an article should be free for everyone to read and take away as their own.

Wikipedia – Example

BUT THE MAJORITY OF the publication is where I see locked articles as a bonus for driving subscriptions. And hence, it doesn't make me happy.

I love Wikipedia and Brain pickings websites. Both of them doesn't restrict their content for anyone. But they need money. So they have a donation button. Which can be used by anyone to donate monthly or one-time money.

And boom, you earn money without restricting content. Brain pickings is an example that an individual can do this. And Wikipedia is an example that this can happen on a massive scale.

When your content creates value for people, a few fortunate will come forward to support it so that the blog stays online. And when you are making your content public, many people can benefit from it. The only criteria for finding your content should be that the people searching should be online.

That's it. The economic background shouldn't decide if they can have access or not. Because we have enough and frustrating experiences of such things in the offline world, too many to count.

The principle is what that matters – as long as enough fortunate members chip in, everyone benefits. And the average benefit increases helping everyone.

The Future – Collaborative Publication

A BOOK STORE IS A FASCINATING place, you as an author don't compete with other writers. When someone buys a book, they are more likely to buy another one too.

So, it's not you vs others, it's you and others in the game together.

And I think the future is in the same direction. There won't be big companies or mega blogs with lots of fans. Rather it will be many small blogs connected to each other. And often promoting others. It would be a big collaborative effort.

For example, the blogs would be connected via a directory or publisher. And there will be many publishers. You can search and find any blogs via the publisher and subscribe to them. Regardless, the content is free, you are showing a way to support it.

And then there will be random suggestions below every article or so about 3 relevant publications or blogs. And slowly, it will become a tight place for blogs to thrive.

Also, it should be easy for new people to join and get support. Once, this happens, it would be a win-win for everyone. Because the collective audience will decide who will get how much money and that too after giving every blog a fair chance.

Companies Need To Align By Being Good

RIGHT NOW, MOST COMPANIES are advertising hard. They throw up the money and boom the leads come in. But that won't be the future.

If you are a company then either you need to start your own blog or some content service so that the audience can find your stories. And then you can share your new products or services on a regular basis with your fans.

Or maybe, connect with a publisher which will act as a niche and then allow all the blogs under them to connect with the brand, if they want.

In either way, the quality of the promotion should be controlled. And it can be because there is no financial incentive for blogs or publishers to resort to cheap tricks. In short, you need to play by the good rules. And everyone deserves the chance – that's the democratic way of doing things.

Internet was made for this and it will thrive to its maximum potential when these things are at their core values.

Most compromising happens because of a desire to earn a quick buck. Eliminate that and you have got a winner system.

Start Now

THE MOVEMENT HAS STARTED. There are many players like Revue and Substack which acts as a publisher. And blogs have subscriptions under them. But there is locked content – I hope that changes.

Also, there are many self-hosted membership solutions available. And it is promoted. Many newspapers are leaning towards supporting themselves with their fans. Because ads are trickier and unpredictable.

Writing, in general, is improving. Because when you don't have to focus on more eyeballs, you stop writing unnecessary clickbait titles.

And you focus more on quality than quantity. Because you already have enough attention, why screw it up.

Regardless, now is the best time to start a blog – either self-hosted or on a publisher account. The landscape is changing rapidly. Get your feet wet now and live the transition of the future of written content.

Your Response to Customer Alters The Future

It is easy to walk down the road and not help your fellow citizens. Because you don't care – it's not someone you know or not someone from your family. This ain't a personal matter so why invest the time, energy and pain.

But when the tables get turned and you find yourself in a situation, any kind of help is appreciated and hoped for.

Of course, the bystander effect comes into play. But for many people, it is too much to do in a tough situation. You don't have to go all out for every situation – but the best you can do is stand and ask if any help is required. And if you can help in any way, do so. If you can't help then do some basic things like calling the family members, ambulance so that she can get the necessary help.

Passing the ball is a fun game. You pass the ball and when the music stops, whoever has the ball will sing or dance.

But in real life, you pass the ball as in the problems to someone else. When a customer comes to you with a problem, you will say – it's because the internet is down or the customer did some mistake or it ain't the right department.

You try to find everything to pass the problem ball to someone else. So that you can be relieved. It isn't a process to provide help or a solution. But rather a mandatory thing to get done with – the easiest thing to do is pass it on.

Pain

WHEN YOU ARE IN PAIN, you want it to go away fast. You don't want to know about the fault, how it happened or what could have been avoided.

You just want the solution asap. Similarly, when you call customer service for a defect in order, you want to get a refund or replacement. If the customer service girl tells how you are at fault and how you should have taken care – chances are that customer will get more frustrated.

So as a good customer service representative, you need to address the problem asap. Once the customers are happy with the resolution, give some pointers on how to improve the experience, what the customers could have done to avoid that and so on. The problem at hand should be solved first.

Because delaying the solution will make the pain hurt more. And by the time you reach a solution, the pain would have been too deep.

Thus the experience might get hampered. You want to bring in peace first and then do whatever you want second.

The Customer

WHEN THE CUSTOMER CALLS for pain, put the onus on yourself to solve the problem. The customer is already frustrated – if you tell her a thousand steps to resolve the issue then chances are you are doing a disservice.

You are being called for fast action and something to please her from the discomfort. And not add anything more to her pain.

Take the high ground, resolve the issue and make sure the experience is smooth. After a problem arises, the customer service should be more empathetic, quick and flexible so that the customers stick and have a fulfilling experience.

And if you aren't looking to do that then don't be surprised when customers talk bad about the experience, don't refer and you find it difficult to hold the high ground.

This of course doesn't mean that you do whatever the customers say. It is quite the opposite – you do as much as you can for the customers that deserve your attention because you want them, customers, for a longer duration.

How To Use Empathy While Doing Customer Service?

CUSTOMERS ARE THE BACKBONE of your business. If you want to start a business then you can either do all the non-essential things like designing your office, renting a big place, doing fancy meetings and so on.

Or you can get your first customers. Because once you have people paying for your product or service then you have a business.

The first part of a business is to get the customers. But the next and most crucial part is to keep the customers for a long time, ideally a lifetime.

Thus, you get a recurring, steady source of income. Also, because of your trust built over the years - you can sell tangential products and increase your revenue.

And guess what, your satisfied customers are the best source of advertising. You can pay for expensive hoardings on blogs or physical stores and expect a tiny conversion. Or you can wow your customers and they will bring you their friends and family as your new customers. Hence, the process looks like this - you sell your service, customers use them and if they want some help - you deliver it above their expectations. And you have an awesome business.

Cost-Cutting

IN EVERY BUSINESS AFTER a certain time, the management does the analysis. To see where the money can be saved.

And often it is decided that serving the customer after-sales is a waste of time. That's why you have an automated machine answering for customers. And a huge long wait if you want to speak to a human being.

This is saving money in the short term. But losing money in the long-term. When your customer service experience isn't human, then there doesn't form a connection.

And if something cheaper comes along or a little better service, you lose out on customers.

At that time, you won't know why they are leaving. But if customer sticks with you despite terrible or bad customer service then you are lucky. However, the internet has accelerated how things will be done. Sooner or later, a better values company will pop up and you will have no time to make amends.

Instead, you should do the opposite. Invest heavily in areas where your customer interacts with your brand. At the initial sales time and after-sales service.

A simple example is when car dealers pay poorly to people at forefront of car sales. Instead, they should be the ones who are paid handsomely, trained and incentivised to have the best customer experience.

A Simple Loop Of Customer Service

MAKE IT SUPER EASY for customers to access you and get a feel for your product or service. Answer all their queries. Be persuasive but not forceful.

And if you find that they aren't an ideal customer, be open to letting them go to the competitor. In fact, help them. This will make sure that you know what your brand stands for. And your product or service isn't for everyone. You will do everything to help if you are the right customer. And if not, you will guide them to a possible better solution.

The next big thing you should do is make it easy for your customers to cancel their subscription if they want.

And your customer service should have a FAQ and common queries page. But if a customer wants to speak to a human, they should be routed asap. Ideally, within a minute of wait time.

When you are angry because of something not working, you need a human touch to let yourself out, be calm and collect yourself.

'Dial 1 for refund' just doesn't do the job. The below conversation does magic for customers in pain.

Customer: I need a refund.

Customer Rep: Sure, I am processing it. May I know the reason for it?

Customer: It's not working, I don't want you sorry, just give me my money back. (Very angry tone)

Customer Rep: We understand how it feels, I have processed your refund. And for your trouble, we have issued a $5 extra refund. Thank you for doing a service with us. If you need more help, we are here.

This is an example of an extremely angry customer. And how you handle things. For most customers, you will get a reason. First, resolve what they want. And then communicate to the product team to fix the issue they had. If you find they weren't the right customers, reiterate to the sales team to not sell to everyone.

Some Pointers Of Great Customer Experience

- Customers can easily reach a human customer rep.

- No metric for how much time you spend with customers - each one of them is unique. Spend as little or as long time a customer wants.

- Refunds processed quickly.

- No matter how absurd a query might seem, you try genuinely to help.

- No funny charges were added via tricks.

- You don't cater to everyone - you know your potential customers.

- If there is delivery, it's as fast as it can be.

- You pay well, train and have a community of employees such that your brand interaction is awesome with each one.

- If someone buys their product for someone they love - and they die. You don't cite your refund policy date is over. You act human.

- You don't give discounts to new customers and lock your previous customers at high rates.

YOU AREN'T IN THE BUSINESS of fooling and taking the money. You do a great service, form a connection and take a fair price.

Go and create something on the internet by learning something on the internet and make your dream come true.

Don't miss out!

Visit the website below and you can sign up to receive emails whenever Rohan Bhardwaj publishes a new book. There's no charge and no obligation.

https://books2read.com/r/B-A-NNCL-XVZRB

BOOKS2READ

Connecting independent readers to independent writers.

Also by Rohan Bhardwaj

This Is Internet
The Big Bang Theory, Black Holes and Beyond Universe
Become Better In Mathematics
A Bend In Marketing : Select Marketing Insights From Seth Godin
Million Dollar Creator Economy

www.ingramcontent.com/pod-product-compliance
Lightning Source LLC
Chambersburg PA
CBHW070139230526
45472CB00004B/1600